PRAISE FO

F(

It is a courageous blessing that Fanta Ballo wrote down all these things she never got to *say*. On every page of her debut collection I am blown away by her tone and tenacity, her valiant rhythm and daring vulnerability. This book is an invitation to us all as she leads by example to learn to stand in herself and her voice, and begin to understand the true power she has in being exactly and wholly who she is. In each piece she is lionhearted in her defense of justice and understanding, making gutsy and expansive choices in her subject matter, in what she chooses to consider, and in the way she takes up space in this world.

- Corey Ruzicano,
mentor and author of *still*

"For All The Things I Never Got To Say" is an affront to those who would seek to silence or marginalize young people. It is a love letter to blackness, queerness, and all of us who believe that being fully expressed is a form of resistance and self-acceptance is a pathway to liberation.

- Torya Beard
executive director at abroaderway and friend

When I read Fanta's work I'm brought back to a time of discovery. A time of exploration. A common lived experience. A time of firsts. With each poem, I'm made to face uncomfortable truths and examine how those moments shaped who I am. Each piece feels like it was written to make us confront the things we have let fade to back of our memories. This is a collection of reminders and never forgets. Fanta's story deserves to be read.

- Shihan Van Clief
mentor and award-winning poet

I've known Fanta since she was a young girl, she has always had an achingly beautiful way of expressing herself. In "For All The Things I Never Got To Say", Fanta shares a voice so brave and intimate you can feel her pulse pound on every page.

- Idina Menzel
Tony award winning actress and friend

For All The Things I Never Got To Say

For All The Things I Never Got To Say

Fanta Ballo

Mckayla Faye, Carly Miller, Corey Ruzicano

Ratty Reach, LLC

ISBN 978-0-578-89143-9

First Printing, 2021

Publisher: Ratty Reach LLC
Editor: Corey Ruzicano
Cover Art: Carly Miller
Illustrations: Mckayla Faye
Author Photo: Betemariam Gebryes

Order online: www.fantaballo.com
also available on all globally distributed platforms.

To my friends and family,
Thank you for always believing in me

This is my story, but if anywhere it resonates with your story, it becomes ours.

With Love,
Ratty

-

Table of Contents

-
Prologue: Learning 2

One Day I Will Love You

Depression 4
MM: The Scene 6
Big Brother 8
MM: Melody 10
Explaining Poetry to My Dad 11
MM: Wrong 13
beCOMING out 14
MM: The First Heartbreak 15
Footnotes To My Mother 16
If I Was A Love Poet 19
Little Brother 22
MM: Lessons Learned 23
Found 24

-
One Day I Will Love Me

-
Black Babies 26
MM: Bleed 27
My Black 28
MM: Rise 32
Dear Basketball 33
MM: Too 36
Harlem 37
Utopian Dystopia 39
Love & Loss 42
MM: Hard Wares 45
Enough 46
To My Grandmother 49
One Day I'll Love Fanta Ballo 52

Acknowledgements 55

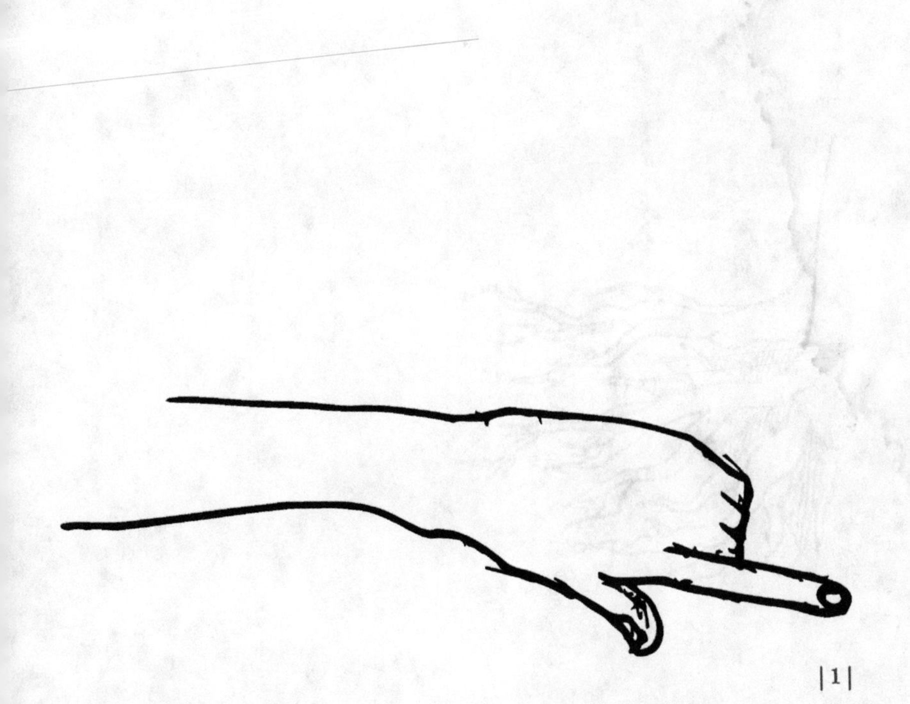

LEARNING

Learning to love myself
must be the hardest course I've ever taken
Learning to constantly believe in myself
on the days where I feel like I won't make it
where I can't take the sound of my own voice

Learning to be at peace with my own silence
Learning the importance of loving out loud
Learning to live for myself everyday
Learning that the learning never stops
Learning that the growing never stops

Evolution is inevitable.

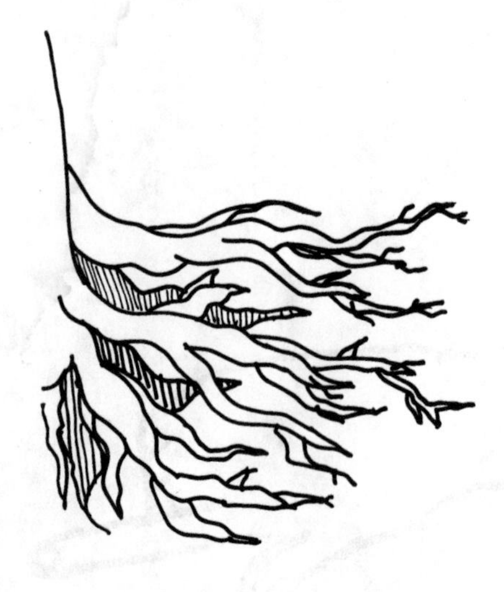

One Day I Will *Love* You...

DEPRESSION

Periodically, I dwell on the days
because there were days,
and many,
where I had to hold myself
reassure myself that everything was going to be fine
then praying every night that I was right

Still there are these days
where depression comes and makes a home in my heart
and anxiety joins and makes a home in my head

I get caught up in the constant battle
trying to figure out who's right
then,
just accepting that they're both wrong

I know there will still be days where
no matter what I do,
I cannot shake the feeling
no matter how far I run,
there will always be those days
with that little voice
calling me back--

You're not good enough
They love you cause it's convenient
But I love you cause you're you
You will eventually fail

Take these wins and stay still

I mistake those phrases for warmth,
the ongoing battle stops for a split second
I am sane,
the waters are calm,
I confuse this comfort for healing
I give in

and even so
I must hope the next time I'm strong enough to run again
my strength will lead me home

MIRROR MIRROR: THE SCENE

It's 2am and for some reason, she's the most motivated in the middle of the night so she rises, goes to the bathroom and stares in the mirror. She's trying to envision what others see when they see her. She speaks. She's mastered the art of words and learned how to speak life back into herself. She's anxious, she has doubts and at any given moment she finds herself staring into the face in the mirror trying to drown out the voice in her head, but she can't, so she decides for once to listen...

I don't know if I'm going to make it big
but I know I'm going to make it out
reminiscing on them late nights,
spending hours contemplating life on my couch
ready to give up
and throw in the towel
after that sudden lapse of judgement
the voice reminds me that

this can't be me
I didn't come this far to lose everything

reflecting on my old days like I can't be beat,
uncertain about my future
but I know it's promising
because there's strength in the struggle
there's passion in the pain
if I ever give up my gift

my life will never be the same

so on the days I feel down,
and I'm just over it
I remember that everything I been through
was just for this moment
and progression is a blessing
as long as you never stop showing up

These are the days I prayed for
no matter how many times I've been knocked down
I have to keep holding up

Honestly my life is on the fast track,
with no sign of slowing up
Nonetheless,
I'm here and I'm alive
and even if I don't make it big
the mirror will know I survived

BIG BROTHER

For Koloba

I spent years in your shadow,
and I spent those years hating it

hated being referred to as the "lil sister"
hated being asked about you everywhere I went
hated being #2
but now I know that that wasn't the case,
I was never in second place
I was just in your shadow long enough
until I was ready to shine on my own

You've been a leader since the day you were born,
I was your first follower,
growing up you was my babysitter
and my second father
You played basketball
so I was eager to pick up the rock
you told me whatever I want to do,
just be confident and don't ever stop

And if I ever fall,
I know I can call on you
Blood made us related,
loyalty kept us tied

I remember the day you told me,
I'll go to war for you

for the first time in a long time
I felt safe
friends they come and go
but my brother, you're here to stay

You was the first born,
you took everything on the chin,
you learned from your mistakes,
so we wouldn't make them again

For that, big brother
I love you

MIRROR MIRROR: MELODY

This voice you've grown to hate,
those around you adore

If I could sing,
I would sing to you every night,
let the melody
chase away the nightmares
and the doubt

Allow your sound,
to be the thing that brings you peace
Brings you,
harmony

EXPLAINING SPOKEN WORD POETRY TO MY DAD

It's like rap
No, no,
it's like a speech
Actually,
it's people talking,
rhyming, and flowing
It's a performance
where instead of claps,
we snap
We replace dancing with listening,
we grasp on each line that rolls off the poet's tongue,
envisioning ourselves in such beauty

Papa,
because of poetry
I have learned to give a part of me
every single time I step on stage
I hang onto miniscule details happening in my life
and create a punchline.
I create metaphors from my pain
and similes out of my grief
My journal has become my best friend,
every major event became a performance

So when I tell you about my poems
and you listen
even though I know you don't understand,
I appreciate your effort

I have yet to find the right language
that creates the bridge separating you and me
I want you to see how beautiful poetry is
but you can't see it *yet*
I want you to feel my pain and understand why I write
But that's a path I haven't crossed *yet*

MIRROR MIRROR: WRONG

I want to love me in all the wrong ways
because love isn't always right

beCOMING out

I was nine when his lips touched mine,
I felt nothing
Ten when he became my *lil baby*
still felt nothing,
didn't catch butterflies,
never felt right

I was eleven when she came along,
my stomach twisted into knots
that couldn't be untied
looked into her eyes
and felt someone could finally see me

I was confused at first,
but the feeling was mutual
A girl liking a girl
some might say unusual
ever since I was young
I've always felt different

I saw that boy,
and felt nothing
She looked into my eyes,
I felt everything.

MIRROR MIRROR: THE FIRST HEARTBREAK

Listen to me,
It will never hurt that much again
your body will adapt
your mindset will shift
your outlook on love will forever be tainted
but never lost
you will love again
next time harder than the first
and you will learn
because that's what Love is all about

FOR MY MOTHER

Momma,
Will you still love your daughter after she is no longer straight?
or
Will you equate your love for me based on who I decide to date?
I know the Quran doesn't deem this lifestyle *okay,*
but I know
Allah created us all by his hand
so by that logic, didn't he make me this way?

I know how happy it would make you
if I portray myself straight for just one day
but it's been 19 years,
and you still can't digest the fact that your daughter is *gay*

I see marriage in my future,
the thing missing is you

Momma,
I already got my suit picked out
debating on purple or blue
I know this is a different lifestyle
something you're not accustomed to

But you brought me here
don't leave me here
cause you're my mother,
and I need you

I'm still the little girl
who got straight A's ,
the one who plays all day,
that little seed you carried for 9 months,
and brought into this world

Yes, I'm gay
but I'll always be your little girl

If I'm being honest,
there's not a day I don't wonder
if my love will lead to the end of our family

To this day I still replay the time
you told me to end it all,
I know you didn't mean it
Still, I wish that I was dreaming

Constantly in denial
I don't want to believe it,
but you told me this when I was 12
again when I was 19 and
some days,
I want to tell you to be careful what you ask for
because you just might receive it

Despite the heartache you caused me,
you're my mother
you don't love how I love,
but I know you love like I love
so I know your hurt is real

Some days I miss your hugs,
and I just want you to hold me
Some nights I miss your voice,
I wish instead of yelling,
that you would've told me

Fanta, no matter what I got you
But, It's already a cold word for black women like us,
so why make it colder?
Even though I disagree, I'll always be your shoulder
to cry on
Cause Allah only gave me one daughter
And I love you

I'll always love you too, Momma.

IF I WAS A LOVE POET

After Rudy Francisco

If I was a love poet,
I would write about how
I don't believe I am good enough for you
how I am not the most religious person,
but something must be up there because
you are heaven sent

If I was a love poet,
I would know the right words to say every time you walk by me,
I would work you all the way up
and then help you with the unwinding,
I would only tell you I love you if I mean it,
because love is binding
I wouldn't throw the word around just cause I feel like it,
I would use it only when I see fit,

only when I see you
and I see it,
our future.

I meant it when I said,
Baby girl you a blessing,
your whole existence is a lesson
you've been strong for too long,
so let me relieve you of your stressing

I know love gets confusing

but I'll never have you guessing,
where my heart lies
You asked me to tell the world I love you
I whispered it in your ear
because *Baby you are my world*

Still replaying the night you sang melodies on my chest
and the sound of your voice
became the only thing that mattered

You stopped me right in my tracks,
to this day
I still replay that sound back
wishing that I could have your voice
on replay and label it my favorite sound track.

When it's late at night
and we're just vibing,
I'll remind you that I love you out loud
and I'll never ever hide it
I can't let this love go
so no matter how long it takes
I'll never stop trying
to figure out new ways to make you smile.

Because love is always worth fighting for
and when I first saw you
my heart played jump rope with my vocal chords
leaving me speechless,
running out of words to say,
jokes to crack,

hoping that at the end of the night
you'll give me a text back

Hoping that at the end of this
my heart will still be intact
and your ex was just a fluke,
this time you won't run back

I know every second of the building is worth it,
Rome wasn't built in a day
so I don't expect us to be perfect
hold my hand and we'll get through this,
no need to be nervous
I promise to love on all your scars,
and every part that's been hurting

I don't ever trip when we fall off
cause I know we're coming back strong
and if you ever forget my love for you,
just come back to this poem

Not enough words in the dictionary
to express how I feel
but I'll never stop searching
and I hope you never will.

LITTLE BROTHER

For Idrissa

I vow to protect you
even on the days where I am not strong enough,
because you stood up for me
on days when I wasn't bold enough
You looked my mother in her eyes
and told her "Fanta is going to change the world"
I've heard that many times,
you actually made me believe it

I still remember that summer
when Uncle decided to give you a haircut,
he shaved your head bald
I cried hysterically at the thought that your hair wouldn't grow
just for it to grow again,
and for me to look like a fool,
in my head I was just being a big sister
protecting you

This poem is for the days I don't tell you I love you,
cause I do
You've grown into a young man
that I haven't quite figured out yet
but I know one thing's for certain,
I got your back until the very end

Little Brother,
I love you

MIRROR MIRROR: LESSONS LEARNED

There will be some nights,
where insomnia keeps you up until 4am
and you will be longing for some sleep
Even if that means nightmares.

FOUND

If I was to lose anyone,
I would hate for it to be you
If I was to love someone,
I would hate for it to be you
because love is taking that leap of faith,
with no safety net,
but with conviction
knowing that at the end,
that inflection in your voice every time you say
I love you
will hit different.

and If you get lucky,
your souls will have intertwined to hum a tune
that will make you scream *I do*
for better or for worse
even if you do it the right way
you can still end up hurt
you know this, you do it anyways
I know this, nonetheless, I pursue
cause if I had to hide from someone
I would hate for it to be you
and if I had to go on searching
I would hope who I found was you.

One Day I Will *Love* Me...

BLACK BABIES

Today you are young. Too young to understand what is going on right now. Why everyone around you just seems sad and depressed. Why your parents are hugging you so much tighter right now. It's because they are scared, they are afraid that at any second an officer in blue can mistake your Black skin for a weapon. That a gang member might confuse your hoodie for Ray Ray's and in any given second you can be taken away from this earth. And some people won't even lose sleep over it. You will always be a Black body first and a child second. You were born a target. To my young Black babies, know that you are strong, even on your worst days. Your life matters. YOU matter. One day, you'll be old enough to understand and hopefully then, things have changed for the better.

MIRROR MIRROR: BLEED

Maybe I bleed,
but I've always ignored the cut.
It's hard to tune out the sound of the leak
so I found the tempo of the drips
and created comfort in it.

Reminding myself,
sometimes you have to sit in the pain
to heal from it.

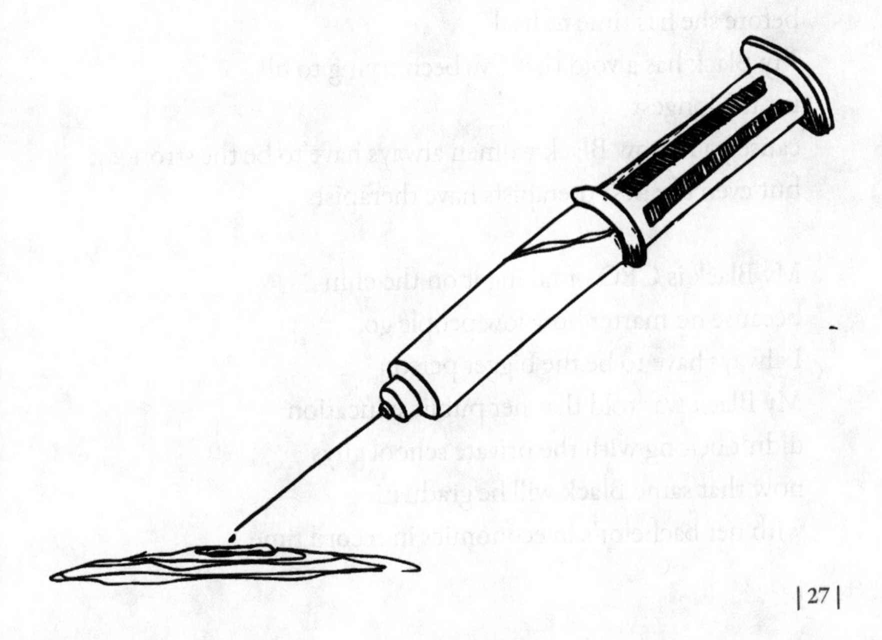

MY BLACK

My Black is not a political stance
you don't get to choose if you want to be red or blue
you don't get to skip out on voting day
just because you want to
My Black is not up for a debate
Being Black shouldn't determine my fate
I shouldn't be scared to die at the hands of police
I shouldn't be squirming every time I hear the chant
I can't breathe
because all I ever wanted was for y'all to see underneath
for police to see more than a target, to see me

Some days my Black just sits and waits for better days to come
not truly knowing if it ever will
My Black is tired of seeing another person die
before she has time to heal
My Black has a void that I've been trying to fill
for the longest
cause you know Black women always have to be the strongest
but even the best therapists have therapists

My Black is CEO of taking it on the chin
because no matter how low people go,
I always have to be the bigger person
My Black was told that her public education
didn't belong with the private school guys
now that same Black will be graduating
with her bachelor's in economics in record time

My Black been defying odds
My Black been breaking records
My Black steps up and steps out
but who cares "how respectable my Black is"
when it will only be highlighted to demean my Black friends
no matter if you are a thug, dropout, doctor or baller
your Black matters
our Black is immortal
our Martyrs will never die
because their name
will ricochet through every twitter chain
while their whole life gets reduced to a hashtag

and I've become accustomed to this story
it's more like a flashback
and I'm tired of carrying the burden
of the "only Black woman"
cause it's one hell of a backpack

My Black takes up space
My Black ain't controversial
My Black shouldn't be tiptoed around
talk about me
talk about how you love my culture
but don't love my pain
how you only care when we die
but don't do anything to change
how you run from our Black
but know every song to our blues
how when we plead Black Lives Matter
you drown us out and say "all lives matter too"

My Black can't be silent
My Black is mad so that's why we riot
My Black has been chained up under the table
which is why my Black is inciting an uprising
and as much as my Black is disrespected
My Black don't discriminate
My Black is open to allies who are down for our fight
My Black knows that all skin folk ain't kinfolk
My Black knows that ain't nothing gonna change
until these institutions do
we need to abolish racism and his cousin colorism too
My Black is the sacrificial lamb
for the Black kin that'll come next
I will take all the bullets
if that means my brother will be able to be Black
a boy and alive
I'll lay my head at the throne of racism
if that means that my brother will survive
the youth
their Black
their melanin that pops just a little more than ours ever could
those young Black kids who deserve to live in a better world
for them my Black has to be enough
that's why I can't let up
I won't let up
so share your mic today
and continue to do so tomorrow
let this be bigger than a moment
let this be a norm
it's time to break out of the system
that you just blindly conformed to

Use your platform to inform those who will only listen
if the words are reiterated by a white woman.

Let them know it's time to wake up
for My Black will never be silenced

My Black won't be overpowered
but My Black is humble enough to know
that alone we'll go fast
but together we'll go farther
so we'll be on the forefront
for this is our movement
but ride for us just as hard
as you ride for our music
and for the love of god
stop talking about the steps you'll take
just step out and do it
the world is watching
and you tell me
What side of history do you want to be on?

MIRROR MIRROR: RISE

Don't be afraid to fall
you can't rise up
if your body never hits the ground

DEAR BASKETBALL,

5,
4,
Shot is in the air
3,
2,
1,
The sound of the ball going in the net
become music to my ears
I fell in love with you because you made me feel safe,
helped me forget about everything else for a few hours,
you grounded me
Things just aren't the same anymore.

I miss you,
I apologize for putting you last
assuming that I would get to you,
assuming that the talent that I had was enough to get me there
I apologize for the practices I missed cause I rather stay in,
For working hard for a week and then chilling again,
For not giving my all when I should've been,
I let you down
I let 11 year old Fanta down,
she had hoop dreams of being on the big screen
didn't expect her run to end at 16
but it did
She was one laid back kid who
didn't appreciate you enough
She took you for granted

Dear Basketball,
I miss you
those late nights in the gym,
those AAU trips with my friends,
the exposure you gave me
you took me places my parents never could,
you gave me experiences that I will forever remember

Dear Coaches,
I'm sorry
I'm sorry for not taking it serious enough,
for not listening when deep down I know I should've.
You went above and beyond for kids
who weren't even your own,
extra practices without pay just to help us grow,
did more for us behind the scenes than we would ever know,
and I took you for granted.
You only wanted to see me win and I didn't really understand it until now
now I see that I was the fool when I talked back,
when I thought I was too good to run those extra laps,
you knew what you were talking about
maybe if I just listened,
this story would've been much different.
I miss the game I love and I'll never get it back again
I see my peers rising up the ranks and I just wish I could go back and try again
cause y'all was right,
someone is always working
even when my clock stopped
those around me were still flourishing

So to Basketball, you gave me life
you implanted a seed of confidence
that helped me come out alright
I just wish I could go back and give you a better fight
but I can't
and even though I miss you, that love will never fade
cause I know you're still changing lives to this very day
you forever changed mine
you are the reason I'm confident with my rhymes,
why I don't get stage fright
because I'm used to the bright lights
you will forever be my glue
even if I'm not on the court,
I'll always find my way back to you

Basketball,
I love you

MIRROR MIRROR: TOO

Being too dark didn't offend me
until I found out
it was supposed to

HARLEM

We are all roses
that stemmed from the cracked concrete;
we didn't need water to grow.

They gave us the end of the stick
told us we won't amount to anything
so no surprise,
they tried to close their eyes,
when we defied every odd in record time
We are at a point where we have to live or survive,
stay strapped up or hide,
put our hands up or die,
put our hands up and we STILL die.

Survival of the fittest,
it seems like our Black bodies just don't fit the mold.
We lose our lives and our stories remain untold.
Against all odds,
we still find ways to succeed in a world this cold.
A lot of my friends took a left,
while I pivoted and took that right.
Even though we took different paths
I still pray they make it home every night.
I pray that when them shots ring out,
they win that gun fight.
Cause we just dealing with the hands we were dealt
and everyone can't win
I'll never blame a brother who got lost in the life of sin

He went with what he knew,
when I decided to look bigger
How he supposed to be "the man"
when he ain't never had a father figure?
How she supposed to level up
when her momma is going through pain?
We were all just little kids,
it was basketball we were playing
When them hoops dreams went left,
that's when they started gang banging
They sticking to the code, loyalty is big with my people
If you walk the walk, you better talk the talk,
cause that lifestyle can be lethal
Same block, same schools, different routes
but at the end of the day
we will always be one
so we gonna figure it out

UTOPIAN DYSTOPIA

They asked me,
how does it feel
to know that you are living in a moment of history?
To be honest at first
it didn't really occur to me
that in a decade from now
my experience will be a topic on the global regents.
They'll have to write an essay about what they read
luckily I can keep my pen to myself
cause I already seen it.
Some days I go to sleep, wake up,
and feel like I'm dreaming.
I've become numb to pandemics, wars,
and disasters happening abroad
I took my life for granted.
Forgot how much of a privilege it was
to live in America
to wake up every day and have an outside to go to
the privilege of breathing in air
fresh enough to keep you alive
parks became the staple
for young kids in the community to play
no one ever questioned the park
cause the park was always there,
school was always there,
food was always there,
we almost always had it good in comparison.
Now that I think about it, it's really embarrassing

we were safe in this bubble
but today we‘re not
Today we realize,
that we are no better than any other country,
we are no better than any other citizen,
the virus is coming for the rich and the poor
yet, the systematic disparities illustrate whose life
matters more.

Years from now,
children will read about this moment
and wonder what it was like for us;
for the people
who lived through a widespread pandemic
The pandemic that made the city that never sleeps?
Sleep
How the things we weren't really grateful for,
became everything we are thankful for
Isn't it funny how we were told
that we rely way too much on technology,
now technology
has become the only thing we can rely on
Having to code switch
between our friends and our professors,
we slide from zoom to zoom like a python

Hearts shatter by millions of seniors
who will not get to commence,
not get to walk down that aisle
and get the honorary paper
that will let them know their years meant something,

them late nights in the library meant something,
them student loans meant something,
cause in all of this
we've seemed to have forgot something
that I am hoping is written in them history books
before anything else we are human,
as scary as this virus is,
it knows what it's doing
reminding us that in the inside we are all the same
we all deserve this thing called life
and if we take it for granted,
it can be stripped away any second.
Life works in circles
I guess that's the roundabout way of saying
one day we won't be here

some of us fortunate enough
to be more than just a statistic
the most famous of us
will have a street or school named in our honor
but the most important won't be those who made
billions and prospered
it will be the ones who lived every day with love
the ones who lend the helping hand to those who
needed it the most
the heroes that didn't wear capes.
It will be the ones that were asked
how does it feel
to know that you are living in a moment of history?
and they will answer
that they didn't really think about it.

LOVE & LOSS

When you lose a childhood superhero,
you lose that legend twice.
When you lose an icon,
it will never feel right,
it will never make sense,
because some things never make sense.

When you lose a superstar,
you lose a role model,
you lose the man that gave kids that look like me hope
let them know there are ways to systematically untie that rope

When you lose an artist,
you rarely bounce back,
You learn to live with the fact that one day we will all be gone
For not even the richest are immortal,
not even the most elite can escape death,
and it humbles you

Reminds you that there is more of life to live
It doesn't matter how tall your tree grows
be happy that it's healthy,
happy that the roots seeded into you are strong enough
to keep you standing tall
on the days where your branches fall,
the cold air knocks your leaves off,
and you're naked, vulnerable and bare

yet still alive.
You still survived,
and everyday that starts to feel more like a luxury in my eyes
What do we do when our heroes die ?
When they say the good die young but I'm still alive ?
when I'm scared to open my phone
cause I might be surprised

with the fact that yet another person lost their life.
and all I can do is say wow,
as I sit back and think that that was someone's child
and they left behind a family
that'll never see them again.

I think about my grief,
wondering if it's misplaced
How can someone I never met physically
get me into this head space?

Where it's hard to get your heart at a steady rate
it's hard to grapple the fact that we all suffer the same fate

Loss has taught me to be thankful
thankful that I made it home to today,
and that flight was just turbulence
cause it could've went the other way
and that cough was just a cold, not the other thing
and that Allah has been patient with me while I find my way

On the days where I feel like my life's a mess,
I take a second and look at how my life progressed

remind myself that even on my worst days,
I am doing better than someone on their best

no matter how dark life gets,
the sun will shine again,
I will rise again,
and no matter how hard life knocks me down,
I'll get back up and try again.

MIRROR MIRROR: HARD WARES

Life became easier when I stopped seeking answers
in places there simply weren't any.
There's no point in going to the hardware store,
looking for lemonade
it will never be there
no matter how bad I want it to be.

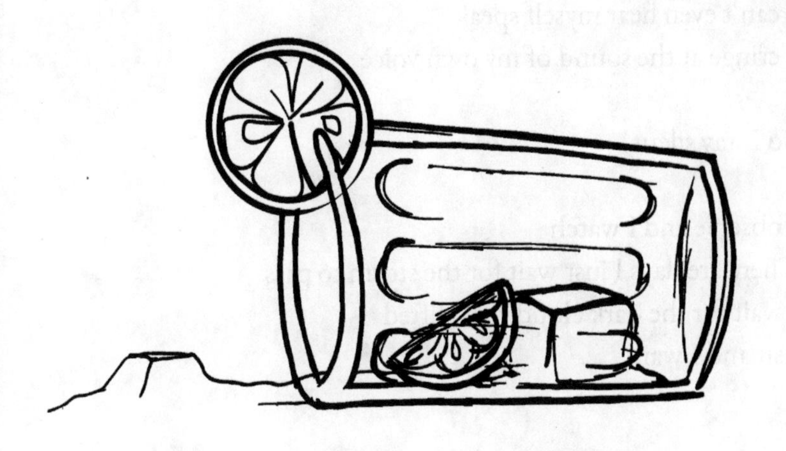

ENOUGH

There are days where I feel like poetry is not enough,
days where writing is not enough,
where I can't find the courage to pick up a pen
because the thought of me doing anything but laying here
is exhausting.

There are days I am exhausted.

There are days I just want someone to hold me and not let go.
To ask me "how are you feeling" and actually care.
There are days where I feel like I am existing but not living,
where I am breathing but barely alive.

There are just days when poetry is not enough.

Where my words are not enough
to bring me out of this cloud of darkness
Where I am so lost in my own thoughts
I can't even hear myself speak
I cringe at the sound of my own voice

So I stay silent,

I observe and I watch
There are days I just wait for the storm to pass
I wait for the dark cloud to be lifted
I sit and I wait

I wait for the days where poetry is enough.

Where my writing is enough
Where my words are enough

The days where I can love again
Those days where poetry makes me feel again
Where the rhythm of my fingers tapping my iPhone screen
calms my nerves
Makes me feel like I am actually worth something

The days where poetry is my healing,
swaddling me up and sitting me on their lap,
my head on its heartbeat like my mother used to do.
Where poetry makes me feel safe

When it lets me write all over it a
and never judges a single thing that I have to say
When it rubs me on my back and tells me
it's fine you were made this way
When it makes me feel big in a world that is huge

Reminding me to take up space within myself
but always leave room
for growth

There are days where poetry makes me forget the heartbreaks,
sings to my soul so I can heal my heartaches

There are days where poetry never leaves,
there are days when it actually stays

Poetry is my safe
Gives me the ability to say what I feel
so everyday,
I sit and I wait,
reminding myself that one day I will see...

Poetry is enough.

Writing is enough.

I am enough.

TO MY GRANDMOTHER

They said that when you lose someone on earth,
heaven gained an angel.
They said as much as it hurts,
you have to look at it from a different angle.
Everything happens for a reason
I shouldn't let your death go in vain,
but ever since the day you left me here,
I haven't garnered up the right words to say.

I lost my mothers mother,
the woman who made my momma woman enough to raise me,
the woman who even on my worst days,
took a second to praise me
last time I saw you I was 11 years old,
I still remember all the funny stories you told me,
about how my mother was so scared of a frog
that she busted her face in
you made me vow never tell her
so I kept that secret sacred
I wish I could see you again
like face to face and face it
that you are never coming back
and I have to take it.
It's just I be missing you everyday
on a daily basis.

I know you're looking down on me,
and some things you won't agree with.

I know I'm not perfect
I'm working on being a better Muslim,
and for you, I'll achieve it.

I was born two days after you,
that's no coincidence
I was named after you too,
that's no small insignificance
We were connected more than I will ever know
I know that because of your spirit,
I will forever grow

If money wasn't an issue,
I would've visited every summer
Maybe if we had money,
I wouldn't have to wonder
as much
I wouldn't have to wander
as much

I'm still piecing together my thoughts of you
from when I was a little girl
When you held me every time I got sick
and always had the right remedies to help me heal.

You would make me Aloko
cause you know how that made me feel
Even though it sucks I'll never see you again,
I'll never get tired of asking again and again,
about you
It's been almost a decade and I still can't forget

about you,
that's why this poem is about you,
in the end, every poem is about you
cause I wouldn't be who I am without you.

ONE DAY I'LL LOVE FANTA BALLO

After Frank O'Hara

One Day,
I'll be able to sing my praise
so loud that they'll always remember my name
and never forget my face,
I'll leave an imprint
My journey to this moment has been long
but I've enjoyed the distance

I've loved and lost people,
every time I grieved different
Born a Black body in a white world
so I'm not ignorant to the fact that I'm perceived different

One day I'll love my gentle heart,
I'll accept that I live with my heart on my sleeve
no matter how much I try - I care
I leave every situation a little less full
because I give,
I give sometimes more than I can afford
but I do it
because I that's all I ever wanted

One day I'll love the crooked smile
momma never had "braces money" to fix
I'll love the way I awkwardly laugh
when I'm nervous

or didn't hear you speak
too anxious to ask you to repeat
I smile
For a while that got me through
Masking my pain with metaphors,
I fell in love with the pen
Found a home in my journal
that's how this journey began

One day I'll find the courage
to put the pen down
actually say everything
I wanted to say but never got to
let this book be my anchor
and stepping stone of faith
Someday I'll love Fanta Ballo
and everything she's got to say.

One Day I Will *Love* Fanta Ballo...

ACKNOWLEDGEMENTS

To my parents: Mama and Papa, thank you for raising me into who I am today. To my brothers, Koloba and Idrissa, thank you for being there for me every step of the way.

To my friends: Traynise Delaney, Jnaya Diallo, Niakale Sow, Abou Fofana, Lizata Camara, Myriam Fofana, Jadon Cupidon, Ky'Jaun Stanfield, Kevon Burke, Tylah Coleman -Sanchez, Chelsea Haibor, Gary Acevedo, Ashley Woodson, Selena Philoxy, Fatima Lee, Anastasia Davis, Tammy Salgado, Crystal Traverso, Ami Mbaye, Oumou Diallo, Keziya Smith, Taylor Richardson, Kemisa Doumbia, Ashanti Dixon, Mary Suriel, Sidika Saliu, Saintangel Acosta, and the many more that I can name, thank you for always being there for me.

To my teachers and mentors: Corey Ruzicano, Shihan Van-Clief, Heather Zuckerman, Marisa Gershwin, Torya Beard, Darren Biggart, my ninth grade algebra teacher; Ms.Gordon, my tenth grade english teacher; Ms.McBean, my tenth grade history teacher; Ms. Melendez, all of my elementary and middle school teachers from P.S./I.S. 76, Dr. Francisca Oyogoa, Dr. Eden- Renee Hayes, John Musall and every other human who has touched my life in some way, I thank you for seeing me.

To Idina Menzel and every single person at the ABroaderway Foundation, thank you for taking in that eleven year old girl and showing her the beauty of sisterhood and leadership. I am forever grateful.

To Shawn Mendes and the Shawn Foundation, thank you for putting your faith in me and for all of your support to make my first book come to life.

To my basketball coaches, thank you for instilling core values into me at a young age.

To Carly Miller, thank you for the amazing cover art. To Mckayla Faye, thank you for the beautiful illustrations throughout the book.

Thank you to all of the black women and poets who have paved the way for me to be here and thank you to all the people who I didn't name individually. I am so appreciative of every single person who's crossed my path and supported me up until this moment. There would be no book without y'all.

Printed in the USA
CPSIA information can be obtained
at www.ICGtesting.com
LVHW011111231023
761878LV00003B/134